Gladys Ijeoma Akunna, Ph.D., is a teacher, researcher, psychotherapist, and artist with an innovative, pioneering spirit. Combining the power of movement and psychology based on both Western and indigenous African practices, she creates a unique, intriguing perspective that resonates as an authentic, African-centered thinker. Her enlightening conversations, or "akuko iho" in her native Igbo culture, showcase her unique brand of African Dance/Movement Therapy (ADMT), reintegrating integral aspects of the (Africanized) body displaced by mental and emotional stressors from troubling histories. Her emerging holistic practice of nonverbal psychotherapy counterbalances the overbearing influence of Western thought governing African mental and psycho-spiritual health.

Gladys Ijeoma Akunna

PLEASE, ADOPT ME, AMERICA

A Poetic Memoir on Race, Dispossession, and Identity

AUSTIN MACAULEY PUBLISHERS®

LONDON · CAMBRIDGE · NEW YORK · SHARJAH

Ordering Information
Quantity sales: Special discounts are available on quantity purchases by corporations, associations, and others. For details, contact the publisher at the address below.

Publisher's Cataloging-in-Publication data
Akunna, Gladys Ijeoma
Please, Adopt Me, America

ISBN 9798886939002 (Paperback)
ISBN 9798886939026 (ePub e-book)

Cover Art Credit:
Prince Neville Akpobasa
princelee01@gmail.com

Library of Congress Control Number: 2024914360

www.austinmacauley.com/us

First Published 2024
Austin Macauley Publishers LLC
40 Wall Street, 33rd Floor, Suite 3302
New York, NY 10005
USA

mail-usa@austinmacauley.com
+1 (646) 5125767

To my dearest mother and father, Virginia Nwahuzi Akunna (Nee Ogboh), and Micheal Ejike Nwoye (M.E.N) Akunna:

For the strength to stand and fight with my feet and my pen, to learn, to dance, and to write. I am eternally grateful. I stand in awe of your love, courage, and power. You birthed me from hope; the same soothes my journey and lifts my heart each day. With eternal reverence and gratitude, I see you in my eyes, always…!

To my loving and steadfast sibl ngs – beloved children of my mother! You are my loyal companions on this painful and bittersweet journey. Some days I take steps that are lightened and sweetened by my fondness for you, and other days I feel heavy steps that cling to my heels, like the lingering taste of bitter kola. Yet through it all, you stand by my side, I thank you.

To all children born in the presence of war: the air you breathe is choked with the burden of unshed tears and sealed lips. May you find your voice faster than we did.

To all youths and adults, male and female, displaced by the pungent smell of death in the living spaces they call their own, may you find peace in a home that you will fill with the aroma of love and joy.

And to friends, teachers, and mentors who lent their hands and voices to cheer me on. Thank you for shepherding my eyes toward the brightness I see on the horizon.

Table of Contents

Synopsis

I was born in Biafra, a country that was, but now lives in my memories. I have a passion for *akuko iho*, which I translate as *enlightening conversations*. Not *stories* or folktales. There is no such word as story or folktale in my native African Igbo vocabulary. ***Please, adopt me, America*** is an enlightening conversation about survival and resilience. It is history, spirituality, and politics. It is about transitions, cultural connections, bridges, healing, and empowerment. It is a poetic memoir – my journey of traversing invisible boundaries of terror for the self and redemption. It is written in simple, fluid, prose-like language.

Preamble

I stared into the vast space
struggling to stay awake
my eyes on the deserted road
tracing the long-winding trail
my tumultuous
wanderings

In my strained vision,
I might have missed
several familiar turns
in the twists
of the treacherous terrains;
I must have lost count
of the many ordeals,
cascading my fuzzy memory
a torrential downpour

Yet, there are a few
that cling fast
begging, tagging along
refusing to be swayed
from the many thorny seasons
I have been a sojourner
a journey of pain and chaos
unending

like eternity
I have crawled, walked, and now
I am running, running
from the nightmares
stuck fast into the cursed land
chocking my breath
Bad dreams that stole
my childhood and innocence
plundered my virile youthfulness,
and NOW threatening to turn
my twilight
into wasted hope!

I stop for a while
halting the cursed trail
my scorched feet touched
on this land

America!
Am I really in you?

My tired feet beg
for rest
from flights of many weary nights
darkness so deep
threatened to swallow
my aching frame
hiding what is left
of the hope of me,
becoming me!

I have been lost
to the pain and torture
etched deep in my bones
the monsters' echoes howling
in my ears close in;
eyes blazing evil and rot
bullying, threatening
to snatch my confused mind
from my body
desperate for life!

Nigeria!!

I fled from you
land of monsters
Cruel depraved spirits of deceit
feeding fat on sad, hapless ones
they pretend to oversee

Umu nmo ojo! (*spirit beings of perpetual evil!*)

disguised in human flesh
stole and imprisoned the land
that once adopted me

Callous presence of doom
they bled the land
of plentiful harvests.
but served the people
thistles and gravels for meals

Amid plenty
and riches,
oil well of liquid gold
ripened forests, lush and green
they garnished empty stomachs
with sighs and tears;

filled minds with biting pangs
the horror and terror
seasons after seasons
time, and time again
they stoked
the high tides violence
turbulence piled to the skies
they bestrode
the land
wreaking havoc
and decay!

Can you feel
Can you see
or even begin to imagine?
these leaders turned into monsters
all day long, all night long
through the years and seasons

All blind as bats
floating in ominous circles
brandishing cracking whips
over blistered bodies
seeping wounds
and oozing decay

Unflinching
and unfeeling
they held high the whip over
bodies with sunken eyes,
grimacing teeth
protruding!

The lawbreakers
with steely hearts,
and stony eyes
spitting gravel
into our own eyes

They sit over torture and chaos
a daily routine
in the dishonored chambers
of the land

Can you feel
Can you see
or even begin to imagine
my journey
through the tattered earth
exploited for selfish gains?

I know you may not;
I may have lost a good part
of my imagination as well
my tired memory
eager to out
the pain
And who would not
be shut down?
numb the soul;
shut the mind
against the torments
of evil clutches
lacerating the bones?

The vile creatures
of gloom
held me captive
clamped my voice
and smoldered my body
in fire-red oppression!
But I have kept fighting
holding on to strength
listening to the urgent voice within
pounding at my breath
it must be toughened
to stay alive!

My Chi calls within

(*the Divine intelligence in me*)

My chi rises
and I am filled

Nkasiobi (*my failing heart toughened; cooked with age)*
I am full of age
and wisdom

In my *Chi!*
Above the confusion
My Chi warns
my mind stirs
and I know that some things
are not what they seem
that I was not

what they said I was,
whom they said I was
and where they said
that I took my life

My Chi beams,
Light shreds the darkness,
revealing
I was not
who I had become
what I was becoming;
I was not the new name
I had been given
and called

In light of my Chi,
I was repositioned
My perspective shifted
I become aware
I could see
I am no Nigerian!

I am not Nigerian
I was adopted
forcefully,
without my permission
I had no right to refuse
or agree
but what is a human being
without their rights?

Now, I know
what was hidden
in ignorance
my new vision illuminates
many past days ago
I see
where I took root
yesterday
I know where
I took root yesterday
like I know my name!

Ijeoma

The *one on a journey*
through countless
transitions
many cultures

Ijeoma!
The one whose mother
severed her *otubere*

(*her umbilical cord*)

from her body and said,

"*My child, you must go well.*"

The one whose father
breathed upon her head
and said;

"*Daughter, safe journey.*"
Ijeoma! (*Safe journey*)

That is my name;
that is me,
child of *Nwahuzi*,

the gentle, merciful one

like a refreshing stream
that is my name,
daughter of *Nwoye*,

the valiant, enterprising one

like the *Oye* market
of *Ala Igbo (Igbo Land)*

Nwahuzi, my mother
and Nwoye, my father
called me Ijeoma
when I came out of them;
the child and daughter
who arrived on earth

**in the fulness
of the troubles of war!!**

And they also told me
what my *chi* (*The Creative Spark of the Divine*)
tells me
that I am the one
born in Biafra's sorrows
but who must seek
from the famished wasteland
golden pathways
The one who must journey
out of the want and stagnation
and chaos

I am the child
and daughter set forth
into the world for good!

No, I do not belong
to these bad spirits
or the land
they desecrate daily
with rotten excrement!

As a visioner
I try to make them see
the torture and pain worn
like faded ornaments
on haggard faces
torn with sorrow

But the bad spirits;
thought to blind my vision
and cripple me
to stop my journey

They sought
to hold me against my will
like forever!
they thought to hold me,
captive in a strange land

A really strange land
I thought
I knew once
Or they forced
To make me believe
I knew
where I treaded

A land
with many strange people,
Very strange!
The monsters
mapped and carved them
in the sombre colors of servitude
and make them dance
the gloomy
percussions of hate and dread!

I had thought these strangers
that they were close to me,
that we were close
and we blended
like our breakfast pap
we drank
on the bare, hard concrete
But with each passing day,
I saw
we looked so different
and acted strange
From the cold smiles,
hardly touching the heart

engraved on changing faces
like a chameleon
darting eyes
bleary with suspicions
hardly seeing
the one called a neighbor

And they spoke
in many strange languages,
like Babel,
hardly hearing or listening
not knowing
or seeing one another

Now they sit
or run around
in the darkness of their souls
depressed, tormented
drunk with gales of absurdities
Voices of protests jeopardized,
bloodied
at the toll gates
cut down in hails of bullets
and armored tanks
YET
all searching frantically
for any escape route
or a cure!

The Flight

Mourning this strange land
I ran so fast
my shaky legs, heavy in flight
took leave of strange people
I have lived with
For many seasons

Mourning a desolate land,
countless torments
mine for a season.

My legs are on a journey
one of many transitions
in search of my true self
in search of my destiny

The monsters!
They thought to stop me,
Ijeoma;
they thought to stop
my journey.
they thought to stop me;
Ijeoma
the one on a mission,
whose forebears saw her journey
before her feet touched the earth

Daughter of Destiny;
a free soul of *Ala Igbo*!
my *Ala Biafra (Biafraland of my birth)*

They thought to stop me
free-born of Biafra
land of the rising sun

Biafra besieged
by ignorance
and crumbled by hate

Biafra killed
without thought
of me and my kindred
Yet lives on in my mind!

The monsters
they did not know me
these abominable beings
like the malevolent creatures
in the *akuko iho;*
the villain characters
in *enlightening conversations*
of my childhood
Nwahuzi and Nwoye,
shared with me
serenading praise of a universe
fair and radiant,
and just

Ala Igbo, my native land

These ugly ones
they did not know me

But how could they
when I was not from them?
they did not know my name
and could not tell
that I am the one on a journey
to find the self and spirit,
and build bridges to
connect
and bind up a world
falling apart
in waves of
unleashed terror!

But how do they think
they could cage the wind
on a destination?
how do they think
they could stop the journey
the restless flight
visions unfolding
How could they stop
one with a mission of life?

Nwahuzi called me

Ijeoma!
Nwoye called me
Ijeoma!

long ago
in the vision of my birth
they saw my journey,
the winding pathways
of many transitions
the travails and the budding joy
like the petals of the morning flowers

They called me
In the beginning,
when I set foot on earth
and my journey began
they set me off
with one beautiful gift;
a living name tied to their breath
and heart

They set me off on this journey
with heaviness
and tightness of the heart;
tears from the eyes like a flood
overrunning
the blighted gray lands of Biafra
agonizing in death

But they invoked joy and hope
in prayers
for me
to find my place
and all good wishes
in the sprawling fields
of the universe beckoning
I am still on this journey
racing with time
running
from the snarling shadows
in the patch of darkness
of the dawn

I run into the womb
of the morning,
as my Chi breaks forth on me
and smiles
in the tranquil light of day

awakening
my yawning dreams
tucked deep in my bosom
searching for me,
and my fading mind
in my own body
in my place of life!
I escaped
from the vampires
clutching my troubled being
with trembling hands
and breath fainting

America!!!

I run into your arms
in a mindless
awkward embrace
awakening
from an ensnared spell of lingering doom!

You look at me
like an alien
from another space
your doubts and distrust
soaking in
bellying contradictions
many memories you hate to own

You seem a bit nervous too,
you also hate to admit
keeping a watchful guard
like the eagle perched on your head

But you have been this way
for more seasons
than I can ever put together
in my drowsy judgment.
Your eyes,
wide open

never winking, like the wide clouds above
stirs me so deeply
to think,
jostling my crowded memory
craving so badly to rest
at this time

Your gaze
bore into my very bones
almost like you
wanted to shred my being
know every bit of me
and my mission
to your pride land
on this very morning.

My family, *ndi Ala Igbo;*

(People of Igbo land)
Ezi na uno; (both from the home
and the wide, scattered streets)

they would say:

"Oge onye tetere wu otutu yaa" (*Any time*
anyone wakes up, is their morning)

I just woke up
this morning
on your land
America
I woke up
this morning
like my first day ever

I am living
determined to flourish
in the newness of this new day
in my morning.
in this new land
of opportunities
and, perhaps, hidden traps
for the unsuspecting
America!
set on a pedestal
America!

your own very dear land!

You look a bit amused
at my thinking
my reasoning
you did not
expect the answer
the mindfulness
from someone like me
with no civilization
as you say
about my appearance and design

I could tell your subtle prejudice
But this morning
I made a little bit
of sense to you
just a tiny bit
in my judgment

"Are you all right?"
you ask me
managing to sound friendly
at least you could know me
you could know my mission
to your land

"No, I am not."
I stuttered
still dazed
from my dizzying flight
my tear-stung eyes,
fight to stay open
searching out
your face
chiseled in the glow
of the morning.

My Chi,
my new day beamed brighter
on my new morning
my witness
to my new beginning
to yet another transition
on your land
America

"Are you all right?"

I heard you ask me again

"Are you hungry?"
"Are you lost?"
"What are you doing here?"
"How can I help you?"

This barrage of questions
break my thoughts;
becloud my memory.

"How can I help you?"
You try to soften your tone.

I look long and deep
and see you
you look familiar
in light of my new day
and a new vision

And your voice too,
it sounds like an echo
calling me back from my yesteryears
I have seen you before
I know your voice too well
beyond the hollow
echoes thundering back
through the passage of times
I can tell

that I knew you
since yesterday

I open my mouth
I speak
in a voice
I could hardly feel;
hardly call my own
it sounded so unfamiliar
in the falsetto of a trance
coming from a deep place
linking many generations
stretching out before me

You look puzzled
you try to avoid
the intense gaze
of a weirdo
of a woman losing herself

Hoarse laughter
escaped my patched throat
at your scrutiny
I guess you must have thought
that I was crazy
and all you would want
in all common sense
was to let go.
Yet,
you held on to me still
or was it I
who would not let you go?

And as I held on to you
the pieces of thoughts
flowed like a steady stream
in my mind
seeking the truth
and guidance
I make efforts
to gather them from every direction

Anaha ano ofu ebe ekiri nmau
(You don't stand on a spot
to watch the masquerade)

This is what
my people say

I let my mind rove,
gathering
and framing memories
like an excited child
picking *udala* fruits (*my precious African star fruit*)
plucked
by the unseen hands of the wind
I followed its many paths
still holding on to you

I was learning to multitask
in my newfound self,
no one would do this for me
my feet would travel
and my hands would work for me

Slowly but steadily
my bitter mind turns sweet
and my stomach too
nourished by the sparks
beaming within
taste sweet and tingly
like *udala*
my precious African star fruit!

I am happy at last
that I was finding
the hidden bits of me
like I was picking
the star fruits
of my childhood in *Ala Igbo (Igbo land)*
how my mind
longs to be free,
to be at liberty, energized –
and strengthened
by new experiences in life

I could tell
my joy blossoming
at the beckoning
of a new hope
as my mind dived into
history's deep lane

In the belly of time
hidden for centuries
lies my family portrait
shielding Nwahuzi
and Nwoye too
but boldly capturing
all *Papa Nnukwu (my grandfathers)*
and all *Mama Unukwu (my grandmothers)*
I never met
but have seen
in the face
of Nwahuzi and Nwoye.

"Are you all right?"

I heard you ask again.
at last
I found a clearer voice
in the midst
of the multicolored designs

"No, please take me to them
take me to meet them
the people in the portrait
and faces I see now
I know they are in this land
Take me
to see them
today."
I have sought for them
They are my family

and you know them
and I have seen you with them
long before today

I have seen you with them,
they were all bound
and smeared with dread
you ferried them
with great fury
on the long, long burden
of the Middle Passage!
I have seen you
before their eyes
dimmed
with longing and anguish
for family and land,
they would never see again
In their faces,

carried on Nwahuzi
and Nwoye's frames.
I met you in *Ala Igbo*
the land of my birth
a thousand miles away
from this place
we now both stand
you and I
the familiar strangers!

"This is insane you"!
you exclaim,
almost yelling
shaking your head
as if in disbelief.

I know! I agree!
But it is true, or is it not
so true
in the light of history?
I understand too
as I look at you now
face distorted
I see that your face
has changed many, many times
in the course
of our entangled history!

You have changed your face
so many times
It is hard
to keep count
I could keep a collection
of your masks,
masks you have won
many, many times
I could keep your masks
to build exhibitions
of history lessons
good for this land

I have seen you
as the grotesque masks
like those dreaded masquerades
of *Ala Igbo (Igbo land)*
keepers of the moral universe
protectors of the people

You mirrored
and imitated
Ala Igbo masks
But you did not know the *akuko iho*

*(enlightening conversation*s)

of the revered beings
so, you distorted the narrative
fixed it in your container
of paternal control
when you met

ndi Papa Unukwu (*my grandfathers*)
na Mama Unukwu (and my grandmothers)

You stole
and plundered them,
the wealth and beauty
of *Ala Igbo*!
You distorted *Ala Igbo* masks
the ugly exterior that covered
the inward effervescence of beauty
authority and service to the people
in equity and justice

For the wearers
took care of the whole family
treated everyone equally
with respect and goodwill
and kept all and sundry safe

BUT punished all wrong

And you?
you wore them
to hide your ugly mien
and bitterness of heart
when you drove them
mercilessly
through the chilly waters
of death
cast their young
to the sea dragons for gains
and crushed their withered bodies
on this land,
we both stand on today.

I see you shake your head again
in disbelief
like this is a tale from Moonlight
casting long shadows and doubts

but your denials
do not change the history

Your discomfort grows
"this crazy narrative
is getting out of hand"
you intone
barely
above a whisper

I know
I can't believe
these pieces of history
took place
it is really hard
to believe too
but this is a moral blunder
that got out of hand
sustained by mischief and ill-will
for many centuries now

To obliterate my family
write their torturous, laborious toil
tear-bathed, backbreaking
mind-bending
and spirit-crushing
off and out
the pages of history

Now I see
that you are full of regrets
this handshake
extended
feels uncomfortable now

reaching toward the elbow
but you need to hear me out
a voice of history
conscience
and Justice

Besides,
a mad person,
if I seem to you as one
as you make it appear
is also worthy of attention
in *Ala Igbo (My Igbo land)*
"Onye ara nu eche ya"

The madman is at home
in the company of their thoughts.
and everyone's voice
deserves to be heard.

my family would agree
wholeheartedly!

I see you relax
your tout guard,
perhaps the wise saying resonated
appealed to you
"What can I do for you?"
you asked quietly, surprisingly
almost in a sweet whisper
like a lullaby
luring a child to sleep

The sound
of your voice changed
the tone and pitch
and you changed it again
like your many masks

Is this an act
the meaning of diplomacy?
you are at home on your turf
the master of intrigues!

I pull away
from my deep thoughts
to gaze
into your face once again
I thought your face lit up
and I was right.

And your feet
I see them begin a dance
your waist tinkling
and shimmying
as the rainbow in the sky
Like the *Agba wo nmawu* mask,

(*The beautiful one of the feminine form*)

beguiling. enrapturing
radiant as the fountain
of endless youth!
I see you call me to
the dance of complex acts
but I cannot answer this call
without a known purpose

In the dance field of life,
I dance with my age grade
with meaning
and responsibility

I would not be beguiled
I am one on a journey
and this is no time
to engage in the dance of joy
if this is the dance
you called forth

How could I?
my feet are still planted
on a journey

I had not seen
or met *ndi Papa Unu Ukwu (the grandfathers)*
and *ndi Mama Unu Ukwu (the grandmothers)*
and my siblings
my big family
on this land

I see that you are passionate
about your dance of celebration
Not so for me, now
In *Ala Igbo* (Igbo land)
there is always a reason
for a dance

Before I join the dance
in your dance arena
please, take me to them
my family
I want to see my family
I want to be with my family!
"But who are they,
this family of yours
the family you talk about
where are they
on this big land?"
you ask
with a slight impatience

I see you –
you think
think to change
your mask again

I gaze back
in bewilderment

please don't change it now
I wish for all light
and clarity
not the multi-dynamic
flow of boundless
confusion
I wonder
how did *ndi Papa Unukwu*
and *Mama Unukwu*
cope
with your many masks
never getting
to see your real face
season after season

never getting to know you,
the one
behind the many masks
and who uprooted them
from their *Ala Igbo*
to bring them
so far away to live
with you
their strange
strange bedfellow!

You stop the dance,
and change your posture
as if to take your leave
I anxiously
search your face

behind the mask,
unwilling to let you go
"Yes, you know them
my family,
like other members
littered and uncared for
in the cotton and tobacco fields
and sugarcane plantations
in your land and regions
controlled by your kind

you sailed them
to Georgia

to the slave market
to spin money from the fields
and clothe you
with the glory
you have today

You sailed them
to Georgia
they were
at the Dunbar Creek
on St. Simons Island
just yesterday"

But instead of the gloomy fields
to build you more fortune
and gold piled high to the skies
under your cracking whips

laid on their bare backs
they chose the waters
man, woman, boy, and girl,
rich or poor, high or low
they wade through the waters
to return home
to *Ala Igbo (Igbo land)*

You call
the unforgettable passage
The *Igbo Landing (Or Ibo Lancing)*
right in the heart
of your Georgia
but they call it
their gateway to freedom;
the great escape
to *Ala Igbo! (Igbo land)*

My family
overpowered your siblings,
their captors
rather than be made slaves
in your land
America

Then with sorrow swelling
They engulfed
in the memory of *Ala Igbo*
Wade in the rolling waters
to the abode of rest

My family, the free-born
in their native *Ala Igbo (Igbo land)*
paved with their bodies
a clear pathway
in the belly of the deep
Please, take me to Dumbar Creek
in their memory
in homage
to salute
their hearts
heavy as lead
their fearless courage

I look
into your eyes again,
searching for a clue
that you heard me
and believed me
my *akuko iho* (*enlightening conversation*)
that Nwoye and Nwahuzi shared with me
and which I now own

I see a tiny flicker
in your eyes
and I press further
"Please, take me
to my family
I have a message
for them."
They need to know
that one of their own
the one on a journey

has journeyed to see them
with messages from *Ala Igbo!* (*Igbo land*)
I see flashes
of memories
I see your smile
grow big in eyes
with a knowing wink

"Please, take me
to my family, now
take me to their space
where they live
here in this land, America
I long for their welcome
and their warm embrace."

If you cannot go to Georgia,
to Dumbar Creek
for swelling tides
of haunting voices
you can take me
to serene Virginia
to *the Igbo Farming Village*
as you call it
in Straugtam

You built the village
for them yourself
after many thoughtful days
the *Igbo farming Village,*
you named it

to honor
ndi Papa Unukwu
na Mama Unukwu (my grandfathers and grandmothers)
and my siblings' too
for the wealth
they bought you
with their sweat and blood

"Please take me
to see them
and my siblings
I hear the drums calling
there is a village meeting
today!"

"I see,
it will be good
for you to meet them."
you finally say
but I have to prepare
for 4TH of July
The Declaration of Independence
Our Independence Anniversary
It is tomorrow
and your family will be there
you are welcome
to attend the festival
as you know your family knows it.
they will attend the festival
from all over this land
tomorrow!

Your words
slowly sink in
I really can't wait
to see and meet
my family
on this land
America
My heart beats fast
I have been on a journey
in search of me.
but I have found
my family too!

My heart beats faster
do I have my future here,
as my family too?
have I merged with the universe
the global village?

I hear a commotion
interrupting my daydreams

Ogba aghara!
(Pandamonium
Everywhere in this land and spread beyond!)

I see Goerge Floyd's America
and my family choked on their breaths
and engulfed in despair

In and around them
loud flames of protests
devour living spaces
like sun-dried summer fires
blowing the heat waves
across distant lands

A jolt of memory
shoots through my mind
igniting thoughts clashing
in a cacophony

What rights and freedom
did the Civil Rights Movement
and Dr. King Jr.
bring here to all my family
both nuclear and extended
when they are still choked by the neck
and begging to breathe?

I see George Floyd
and the knee of choking
all my family
both young and old,
male and female
choked by the neck
on the hard concrete streets

I shudder at the cascading thoughts
is my family part of this land
do they have a future in this land
where like I
they were forcefully adopted?

I turn to look at you
I see you
looking remorseful
you speak as you
put on yet another mask

"America
is a land
in transition as well
a land of many transitions
in History
a land
trying hard to right wrongs
systemic racism, oppression
stereotypes and chokings
installed for centuries
America is trying hard
to live a good name
in the sight of the world
And there is
the post-George Floyd America
I sincerely hope
of internal reflection,
positive actions,
binding wounds

and spreading opportunities,
equity and justice
as stamped
in the American Constitution!"

My eyes bore into your eyes,
like I want
to tap the truth
from the depths of your being

They only beam hope
like the mask you now wear

Yes, this new mask
it's so regal
it took my breath for a moment.
I looked at the splendor

It is the Majestic Ijele Mask
The king of masks in *Ala Igbo*! (*Igbo land*)

America!!!

The Regal One
with majestic steps in emblazoned footprints like Ijele

I called out in awe
I know that you
also carried with you
a huge part
of the pristine beauty and culture

of *Ala Igbo (Igboland)*
to make up your own
when you took *Papa Ukwu na Mama Ukwu*
(my grandfathers and grandmothers)

You stripped *Ala Igbo* naked
with the conniving
crookedness
of the wicked chiefs
in the land of *ala Igbo*

And today, America!
You stand so tall
in the towering masks
of *Ijele*
shining in the power
of your wealth
built by the toughened hands
of *Papa Ukwu na Mama Ukwu (grandfathers and grandmothers)*
and my many, many siblings

You called them your slaves
but they were free-born
noblemen and women
and happy, vibrant boys and girls,
the pride and future of *Ala Igbo*

You treated them as slaves
without a soul.
slaves, with no past, present, and
also, without future?

You crack another wry smile
almost like a grimace
at the taste of a bitter pill!
"There are quite a lot of families
From around the world
here with me,
But I see whom you meant now"

I know your family well
like the back of my palm
I know
how your immediate family
and members
of your extended family
came to live here
and be called Americans
and remember how
they all came here

And yes, as you call it
your *akuko iho* is true

enlightening conversations
of so many experiences,
peoples and events

I agree
that I treated them
your family badly
as you already sensed and
as they will tell you
today, when you see them
Because I know
that you will give
everything
to be reunited with them
today

"America"!
I called out again
If you have played badly
and treated my family
so horrendously
yesterday
and you know
today is not
so good a picture either.
If you have let them cry blood
from the eyes
And let them see their ears
with their eyes,

Will you as you promised
begin
by telling my family how sorry
you are for your bad acts
and promise
to make things right

and treat my family well
with all the dignity and respect
they do deserve
here in this land?

Will you adopt my family properly
into your large family
like every other family
who has come here
from around the world
and the grand family
we all met on this land
the owners of the land
that you call
Native Americans?
will you adopt them properly
and also treat them
truly well
as your own family
in the only land, they see now?
Still shrouded in *Ijele* masks
I see you
submerged in deep thoughts
as the multi-layer brilliance
of *Ijele*

I hope you come up
with brilliant
and uplifting decisions
to calm the frayed nerves
on the broken minds
and bodies of my family

I wait to hear from you speak
I wait to see you act;
my gaze fixed on you,
waiting to hear you speak
Until then
there's one more request,
and it's about me,
Ijeoma
who was born in Biafra
the country that was
but is no more
only now
seen in my mind's eye

Will you take
Ijeoma
child of Nwahuzi
daughter of Nwoye
born to Biafra

will you take
the one
who took flight
many seasons ago
the one
on a mission
to find herself
and, please,
adopt me, America
as I merge
with the universe?

Thoughts on Please, Adopt Me, America

By Tony E. Afejuku

(Professor of English and Literature and Creative Writing)

The first thing that struck me when I beheld Gladys Ijeoma Akunna's work under my lens was what this new poet calls "Synopsis," a kind of an unusual prefatory stamp that she appends to it, and which reflects what she wants us to see and accept as her concerns in her "poetic memoir." She begins her briefly brief synopsis this way: "I was born in Biafra, a country that was, but now lives in my memories. I have a passion for **akuko iho**, which I translate as **enlightening conversations**. Not **stories** or **folktales.** There is no such word as story or folktale in my native Igbo vocabulary." I was taken aback to hear her say that in her "native African vocabulary" there is nothing like "**story** or **folktale**" as a word. How can this be true? As an African scholar and poet of sufficiently fine and fair reputation, to say so mildly, who is no stranger to oral literature and folklore, even though that is not my primary field of scholarly engagement, I could not but ask this question several times over in a manner of "enlightening conversations" with myself. In any case, there is no African language that has no word for "story or folktale" in its vocabulary. Speaking specifically about Gladys Akunna's native Nigerian (or her ex-Biafran) Igbo language vocabulary, I, being not an Igbo, in order to test or prove the veracity of her statement and claim, put a call to an Igbo scholar, writer and Professor of English Studies of many years standing; incidentally, this literary personage is an oral literature expert who has done extensive research on Igbo oral literature, including its poetry, stories and folktales. I put down here his text message as follows:

'Akuko' in Igbo stands for 'story' of all kinds. Akuko ifo or ihe or iho or iwho (Afikpo/Abakaliki area) refer to the folktale or folk story.

Whatever Gladys Akunna's passion for "enlightening conversations" (which is the context in which she wants us to accept "akuko iho") is or may be, we rightly should read **Please, Adopt Me, America** as a poetic rendition of different aspects of Igbo folktale or folk-story that dwell on diverse experiences which are personal, extra-personal, private and public, communal and historical, political and sociological, spiritual and philosophical with some perspectives of the phenomenological, all of which cohere in Gladys Akunna's memories, and which constitute, in varying degrees, parts or aspects of her pre-occupations in her text. Of course, she wants us to read the work mainly as a "poetic memoir" meaning that the work is also a kind of autobiography in which is gathered and illustrated everything about her "journey of traversing invisible boundaries of terror for the self and redemption." In one word, we may call her poetic journey a journey in which she traversed strange latitudes and longitudes that eventually ended in America her new home, her new land which she as an immigrant wants to remain in forever! Nigeria and the non-existent Biafra of her childhood or girlhood are now remnants of her memories which America, her new mother- or father-country must wean her of as time goes by. Her "Preamble" speaks volumes:

> I stared into the vast space
> Struggling to stay awake
> my eyes on the deserted road
>
> Tracing the long-winding trail
> [of] my tumultuous
> wanderings
> ….
> I must have lost count
> of the many ordeals,
> cascading my fuzzy memory
> a torrential downpour
> ….
> I have been a sojourner
> a journey of pain and chaos
> unending
> like eternity
> I have crawled, walked, and now
> I am running, running
> from nightmares
> stuck fast into the cursed land
> choking my breath

Every imagery, every symbol, every word – plain and un-plain – that "Preamble" contains is that of the liquidator in the liquidating land that Gladys Akunna has escaped from physically, spiritually, psychologically, and emotionally. Her experience in Nigeria before her physical escape or journey out of it is the story of her escape out of home that was not home, the story of home and homelessness which she tells and re-tells in diverse forms and tropes from the beginning till the end of her poetic memoir – which actually, is not a poetic memoir but a kind of poetic autobiography, physical and otherwise.

Clearly, memoir and autobiography are two literary forms that intertwine but are not exactly the same even though they share an intrinsic affinity. They come from the same source which is the creative imagination of the teller of the recounted tale that tends to dwell more on the experiences of others, the collective, rather than on those of the teller. The memoir of the memoirist does not concentrate fully on the memoirist as the autobiography of the autobiographer does. The memoirist thus focuses less on the self and concentrates on other persons and events unlike, strictly speaking, the autobiographer whose main concern is with the self of the teller of the recounted tale. Has Gladys Akunna, the new immigrant-poet, in this her debut poetic rendition of her experiences not done injustice to the term which she has applied to her enterprise? Her journey in poem after poem or from poem to poem tends to lend credence to my observation.

The poem "Nigeria" easily comes to mind here. The poem is not just about her, but about other persons, creatures, who the monstrous system of monsters, the monsters, who are rulers rather than political leaders of the people:

> I fled from you
> land of monsters
> Cruel depraved spirits of deceit
> feeding fat on sad hapless ones
> they pretend to oversee

Stanza after stanza, line after line in the rendition (and other renditions), capture her pains, trauma, emotional incapacitation, and those of others. The horrific setting of the land, of the country, her erstwhile country called Nigeria, is conveyed in tropes of place and time that compel her to come to this conclusion before her final conclusion:

> I am not Nigerian
> I was adopted
> forcefully
> without my permission
> I had no right to refuse
> or agree
> but what is a human
> without their rights?

The poet's personal autobiography shines forth in "Nigeria" in ways that are disturbingly disturbing and horrifyingly horrifying. But it is also the "autobiography" or "biography" of Nigeria and of other luckless Nigerians, who have nowhere else to escape to, who are not lucky to be adopted by America. Through her story, Gladys Akunna portrays and elucidates the repressed but visible fears, mute but keen perspectives, silent but loud opinions, and objectives that go on even within the minds of Nigerians in the diaspora whilst battling with a perfect settlement mentality and responsibility in their new environment where what they expect to acquire do not really meet their expectations. In making this remark I recall tellingly Segun Afolabi's *A Life Elsewhere* and Chimamanda Adichie's, *The Thing Around Your Neck,* two respective short-stories collections by two Nigerians in the diaspora. In these respective short-stories collections we are meant to believe "that the dislocation from one's native land does not only happen physically, [but] it is also ingrained into thought processes and patterns" (Aiyetoro 36-37). While Segun Afolabi and Chimamanda Adichie's respective post-colonial short-stories are entertaining and enlightening fictional mirrors of diasporic characters who are mainly Nigerians (or ex-Nigerians), Gladys Akunna's poetic renditions of her personal experiences and observations, are realistic non-fictional "tales" in which she maintains a convincing and firm sense of involvement, so to say, in an environment and its reality that are both concrete and continuous in her memory, an act and art that give semblance of fiction to her realistic memory.

From this observation, it follows that her memory even in faraway America historicizes the politics and political events that give the shape and order to *Please, Adopt Me, America* in which the poet exhibits a moral, spiritual, and political commitment to interrogate the social, and economic injustices in Nigeria and elsewhere, that is, specifically, America of the recently murdered George

Floyd and of the long gone Dr. Martin Luther King Jr. and his Civil Rights Movement. Of course, in her interrogation Gladys Akunna strives to build bridges of understanding and of compassion and of love across the contentious divides and demarcations of class, culture and race and ethnicity that the poet's beloved America usually and ironically signals. Yet it may be fair to say or to suggest that Gladys Akunna emerges from "Ijeoma," the seemingly artistic epitome of her rendition of self, to the longishly longish "America" of significant historical development as a new post-colonial or diasporic poet who we must subject to hard psychoanalytic analysis.

Biafra is dead yet she is all "Biafran" in her artistic consciousness in "Ijeoma" that she strategically spices with "Biafran" Igbo tropes (as she similarly does in other "tales"). "Ijeoma," her middle name, which in "Biafra"-Nigeria Igbo language means "safe journey," an indication that at her birth/naming in "Biafra" her "flight" to America had been spiritually and historically foretold and referenced. She would write her destiny as ordained by her *chi,* her personal guiding spirit, as a "Biafran." Curiously, however, she is unable to delete entirely from her consciousness her Nigerian identity because she cannot sever her Nigerian identity from her "Ijeoma" consciousness – despite her ethnic wish to do so. The reality of her Nigerian history usually intrudes in her Igbo consciousness, and introduces, quite deliberately, several contrary or discordant elements about Nigeria into her "tales" in order to justify her flight, safely or un-safely, from Nigeria that entirely erased her and her family's Biafran dreams after Biafra's defeat in the 1967-1970 Nigeria-Biafra civil war.

Do we call Gladys Akunna a psychologically confused poet who is not aware that she is so confused or contradictory in her rendition and goal or objective to the essential point of her unawareness of her motivation? To summarize her in this manner may be too severe a judgment. Her poetic autobiography is her justifiable attempt to resolve the conflict that the Nigerian condition induced in her consciousness as a budding writer. As previously said or implied, the monstrous Nigerian condition that idolizes the culture of exploitative ostentation, and of all kinds of oppression and marginalization of the weak, the poor, the downtrodden, the vulnerable, and the vanquished in every conceivable way, engender in her thematic and rhetorical consciousness what she has offered us in ***Please, Adopt Me, America.*** The facts of her African homeland's history were/are compelling enough to turn her, as relatively young as she is, into a demoralized African human who is earnestly pleading to be accepted as an American baby! But the spirit of her plea is actually, after all said and done, that of irony that is acute and deep. In every true or sincere sense, America is not better than Nigeria. Nigeria, in spite of all its democratic, social, and economic problems, is still by far majestically superior to America still seriously lacking in human virtues. America, to boot, is an anti-freedom, anti-human rights, and anti-human country. The poet tells this fact pungently and pointedly:

A jolt of memory
shoots through my mind
igniting thoughts clashing
in a cacophony
What rights and freedom
did the Civil Rights Movement
and Dr. King Jr.
bring here to all my family
both nuclear and extended
when they are still choked by the neck
and begging to breathe?
I see George Floyd
and the knee of choking
all my family
both young and female
choked by the neck
on the hard concrete streets
I shudder at the cascading thoughts
is my family part of this land
do they have a future in this land
where like I
they were forcefully adopted?

The history of the blacks in America is the history of providentially forced adoption in an age when the blacks were infamously schooled, taught, and compelled to believe and accept that they had no filiopietistic history even though they were shipped from Africa, the rich continent, in land mass, thrice the size each of Europe, USA, China, and other countries put together; the rich continent of aeons of rich history the whites omit or gloss over in their accounts in order to perpetrate eternally their exploitation and domination of the people, to put it mildly. Gladys Akunna's African sensibility and instinct cannot but reject this America. Her motive in giving her book the title she has given it is morally instructive and wittily so after all. Her title is clearly optimally meaningful. And the irony of it is lyrically so!

It will be fitting to end this essay with the following quote from the Welsh poet Dylan Thomas (1914-1953):

I read somewhere of a shepherd who, when asked why he made, from fairy rings, ritual observances to the moon to protect his flocks, replied: 'I'd be a damn' fool if I didn't!' (xix)

Despite the aspects of thoughts I have expressed here overtly and covertly in diverse guises about her doubts, confusions, contradictions, sensibilities, and short-comings, Gladys Akunna wrote what she has written as a diasporic or post-colonial shepherd of her African and black flocks for the love and compassion she has for them and for their protection. She empathizes with suffering Nigerians and her fellow Igbo people, and the tormented blacks in white-controlled America that she anxiously and ironically adores but without a crucially obvious praise of the white system – and she would be a "damn' fool" if she hadn't – even though she sincerely or desperately wishes to "merge/with the universe" in America. She is a fair and fine diasporic bard in chains in exotic America!!! My three exclamation marks are as loud as the rhetorical irony of this admirably resilient humanist whose incandescent tropes are as lyrically incandescent as a compos mentis creative composer can be.

Review of Gladys Ijeoma Akunna's "Please, Adopt Me, America"

By KC Ikwuakor (PhD)

(Founder, President & CEO of PEER Research Ltd.)

In her poetry memoir, ***Please, Adopt Me, America***. Dr. Gladys Ijeoma Akunna weaves the narratives of a perpetual world sojourner who has undergone pains and chaos to be where she finds herself today- in America, journeying from the land of her birth, Biafra. Even though Biafra ceased to exist many years ago, she still envisions Biafra as the cradle of her existence, motivation, comfort, and spirituality. She disowns Nigeria, her country of citizenship, and calls it a land of "monsters" and "vile creatures", a strange land from which she has escaped. Thanks to her "Chi" that provided the enlightenment and her parentage that, providentially named her "Ijeoma"- the one on a journey, "sent forth into the world for good".

Her journey has brought her to America, a journey that was triggered by the rottenness in Nigeria and catalyzed by her quest for space and relative freedom that would enable her to achieve the objectives of her journey.

She is unmindful or undeterred by the different masks America has worn through its history- including slavery, racial discrimination, and political machinations. While

America may not be her final destination, in terms of location, it is a place where she finds solace and special affiliation because of the bravery, courage, and contributions that her Igbo ancestry, as well as the contemporary Igbo generation, have made in the building of America. And because she feels she can also contribute, and America can achieve the majesty and royal stature symbolized by her native Igbo, "Ijele Masquerade", she is emboldened to seed American adoption.

Please, Adopt me, America!
By
Gladys Ijeoma AKUNNA
Review Comments By *Charles Nwadigwe Ph.D.*
(Professor of Cultural Aesthetics and Entertainment Technology)

Gladys Akunna's **Please, Adopt Me, America!** is an autobiographical explosion of both spontaneous and bottled-up emotions. Akunna leads us on a journey through a maze of historical and psychological encounters and finally berthed at Uncle Sam's harbor. Indeed, the journey motif reverberates through the composition with powerful allusions to the poet's traditional Igbo name, *Ijeoma* – a name laced with metaphorical semiology. On one hand, *Ijeoma* wishes the traveler a safe trip; on the other hand, it celebrates a triumphal arrival.

Having taken 'flight' from the vicissitudes and frustrations of the motherland, and landed in the New World, the poet is submerged in a sea of contradictory emotions and ambivalent imageries: relief and nostalgia, jubilant expectation and cautious optimism. But Akunna's plea for Adoption by Uncle Sam is not from a beggarly position of an undocumented economic migrant or embattled refugee. The poet demands Adoption with a sense of entitlement because the labors of her forefathers who survived the Middle Passage turned the wheels that built America. Hence, like Lenrie Peters in his popular poem *We Have Come Home*, Akunna has also "come home", either as prodigal returnee or reincarnate of Dunbar Creek hero(in)es of Igbo Landing.

A lovely collection.

– Emille Bryant

A well-written piece.

– Professor Appolos Okwuchi Nwauwa

It is structurally good ...it speaks to the feelings of any Igbo person living in the diaspora and encapsulates the questions, thoughts, and reminiscences of Ndigbo of deep critical thinking in the diaspora. Excellent work.

– Professor Chijioke Uwah.

Works Cited

Adichie, Chimamanda. *The Thing Around Your Neck.* London: Fourth Estate, 2009. Print.

Afolabi, Segun. *A Life Elsewhere.* Lagos: Farafina Books, 2012. Print.

Aiyetoro, Mary Bose. "Exile and the Making of New Homes in Segun Afolabi's *A Life Elsewhere* and Chimamanda Adichie's *The Thing Around Your Neck. Papers in Linguistics (PEL)*, Nos. 3 and 4, Sept/Dec. 2023. 33 -59. Print.

Thomas, Dylan. *The Collected Poems of Dylan Thomas* (Introduction by Paul Muldoon). New York: New Direction Books, 2010 Edition. Print.

www.ingramcontent.com/pod-product-compliance
Lightning Source LLC
Chambersburg PA
CBHW061352140726
47997CB00003B/1164